Tessa has a new carpet.

There is some left over.

"Can I have that?" says Ben.

"Yes," says Dad. "What for?"

"Aha!" says Ben.

Sam's mum puts an old jug in the bin.

"Can I have that?" says Sam.

"Yes," says Mum. "What for?"

"Aha!"

Jojo and Mouse see a skip.

A man has come to take the skip away.

"Yes," says the man. "What for?"

"Our secret room looks good," says Ben.